FUN FACTS ABOUT
LIZARDS!

W9-CAW-406

Carmen Bredeson

Enslow Elementary
an imprint of

E | **Enslow Publishers, Inc.**
40 Industrial Road
Box 398
Berkeley Heights, NJ 07922
USA

http://www.enslow.com

CONTENTS

WORDS TO KNOW

chameleon (cuh MEEL yun)—One kind of lizard. It can change the color of its skin. It can move one eyeball at a time.

gecko (GEH koh)—One kind of lizard.

hatchling (HACH ling)—A baby animal that comes out of an egg.

PARTS OF A LIZARD

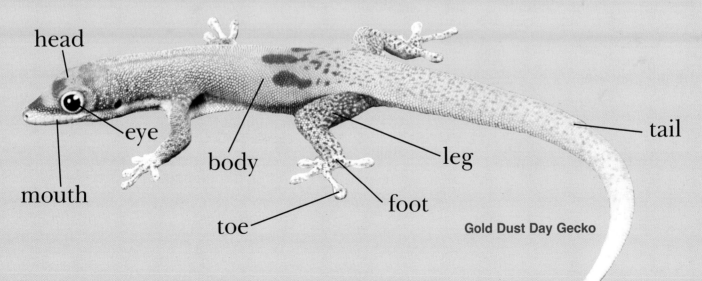

head

eye

mouth

body

toe

foot

leg

tail

Gold Dust Day Gecko

3

4

Lizards live in many places around the world.
They live in deserts, swamps, and forests. Some live high in trees or deep in the ground. Lizards like warm places best. They do not live where it is very cold.

WHICH IS THE BIGGEST LIZARD? WHICH IS THE SMALLEST?

The Komodo dragon is HUGE! It can grow to be 10 feet long and weigh 300 pounds.

Yellow-bellied House Geckos

One kind of tiny lizard will fit on the end of your finger. Most lizards are about as long as a hot dog.

Komodo Dragon

This chameleon catches an insect with its long, sticky tongue.

WHAT DO LIZARDS EAT?

Small lizards eat mosquitoes, cockroaches, worms, and spiders. Bigger lizards use their strong jaws to eat mice, birds, and eggs. The Komodo dragon also eats deer, goats, and other animals.

A Desert Agama eats a scorpion.

9

WHAT EATS LIZARDS?

A snake slithers across the ground, looking for a lizard to eat. A bird swoops out of the sky and grabs a lizard from a tree branch. Owls and cats also like to catch lizards for lunch. *Gulp*.

This snake in Africa is eating a chameleon.

Frilled Lizard

HOW DO SOME LIZARDS FOOL THEIR ENEMIES?

Chameleons change colors to hide. They can turn green like leaves or brown to match tree bark. The frilled lizard spreads out a ruffle around its neck. This makes the lizard look too big and scary to eat.

Flap Neck Chameleon

13

DID THAT LIZARD JUST LOSE ITS TAIL?

Some lizards have a great trick. When an enemy tries to attack, the lizard's tail breaks off. The tail keeps wiggling while the lizard runs away. The enemy thinks it has caught a live animal, but it has caught only a tail. The lizard can grow a new tail.

Blue-tailed Skink

14

This lizard is growing a new tail.

Green Anole

Jamaican Crested Lizard

16

WHY DOES A
LIZARD
LOSE ITS SKIN?

Lizard skin does not grow like our skin. As a lizard gets bigger, its old skin gets too small. New skin grows and the old skin falls off in pieces.

Iguanas

HOW DO LIZARDS CLIMB SO HIGH?

Most lizards have claws on their toes.
The claws help them climb trees and high walls.
Geckos have tiny hairs on their feet. The hairs hold tight, even to glass. Geckos can crawl across a ceiling without falling down.

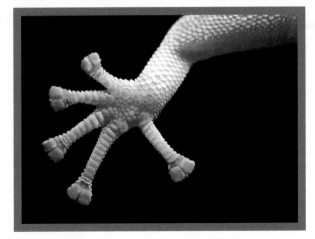

Gecko foot

WHAT IS THE LIFE CYCLE OF A LIZARD?

1. Mother lizard lays eggs in a nest. Little lizards grow inside the eggs. Each baby has an egg tooth to help break open the egg.

2. Out pops the little lizard. It is called a hatchling.

3. This collared lizard is all grown up.

LEARN MORE

BOOKS

Eckart, Edana. *Komodo Dragon*. New York: Scholastic Press, 2003.

Facklam, Margery. *Lizards Weird and Wonderful*. New York: Little, Brown and Company Children's Books, 2003.

McCarthy, Colin. *Eyewitness: Reptile*. New York: Dorling Kindersley Publishing, Inc., 2000.

Australian Thorny Devil Lizard

WEB SITES

Enchanted Learning

<http://www.enchantedlearning.com/subjects/reptiles/lizard/printouts.shtml>

San Diego Zoo

<http://www.sandiegozoo.org/animalbytes/t-lizard.html>

Smithsonian National Zoo

<http://nationalzoo.si.edu/Animals/ReptilesAmphibians/>

Small-scaled Wonder Gecko

INDEX

Veiled Chameleons

A Note About Reptiles and Amphibians:

Amphibians can live on land or in water. Frogs, toads, and salamanders are amphibians.
Reptiles have skin covered with scales. Snakes, alligators, turtles, and lizards are reptiles.

Enslow Elementary, an imprint of Enslow Publishers, Inc.
Enslow Elementary® is a registered trademark of Enslow Publishers, Inc.

Copyright © 2008 by Carmen Bredeson

All rights reserved.

No part of this book may be reproduced by any means
without the written permission of the publisher.

Library of Congress Cataloging-in-Publication Data

Bredeson, Carmen.
    Fun facts about lizards! / by Carmen Bredeson.
        p. cm. — (I like reptiles and amphibians!)
    Includes bibliographical references and index.
    ISBN-13: 978-0-7660-2789-3
    ISBN-10: 0-7660-2789-9
    1. Lizards—Juvenile literature. I. Title. II. Series.
QL666.L2B82 2007
597.95—dc22   2006015917

Printed in the United States of America

Paperback ISBN 978-0-7660-3596-6

Every effort has been made to locate all copyright holders of material used in this book. If
any errors or omissions have occurred, corrections will be made in future editions of this
book.

To Our Readers: We have done our best to make sure all Internet Addresses in this book were active and appropriate when we went to press. However, the author and the publisher have no control over and assume no liability for the material available on those Internet sites or on other Web sites they may link to. Any comments or suggestions can be sent by e-mail to comments@enslow.com or to the address on the back cover.

Photo Credits: Cover, 24 Digital Zoo/Stone/Getty Images; p.1 Matej Kastelic/Shutterstock.com; pp. 2, 8, 18 Stephen Dalton/Science Source; p. 3 JH Pete Carmichael/The Image Bank/Getty Images; p. 4-5 Auscape/UIG/Getty Images; p. 6 © Hanne and Jens Eriksen/NPL/Minden Pictures; p. 7 Reinhard Dirscherl/WaterFrame/Getty Images; p. 9 blickwinkel/Alamy; p. 11 Anthony Bannister/Science Source; p. 12 © Dave Watts/Alamy Stock Photo; p. 13 © Murray, Patti/Animals Animals; p. 14 Waina Cheng/Jupiter Images; p. 15 Leena Robinson/Shutterstock.com; p. 16, 20, 21(2) © Leszczynski, Zigmund/Animals Animals; p. 19, 22 Shutterstock.com; p. 21(3) USFWS/U.S. Fish and Wildlife Affairs; p. 23 Animals Animals/Superstock.

Series Science Consultant:
Raoul Bain
Herpetology Biodiversity Specialist
Center for Biodiversity and Conservation
American Museum of Natural History
New York, NY

Series Literacy Consultant:
Allan A. De Fina, Ph.D.
Past President of the New Jersey
    Reading Association
Professor, Department of Literacy Education
New Jersey City University
Jersey City, NJ